BODY
&
SOUL

JAMES RUSSELL

Newton-le-Willows

Published in the United Kingdom in 2019
by The Knives Forks And Spoons Press,
51 Pipit Avenue,
Newton-le-Willows,
Merseyside,
WA12 9RG.

ISBN 978-1-912211-26-5

Copyright © James Russell, 2019.

The right of James Russell to be identified as the author of this work has been asserted by them in accordance with the Copyrights, Designs and Patents Act of 1988. All rights reserved. No part of this publication may be reproduced, stored in a retrieval system, transmitted in any form or by any means, electronic, photocopying, recording or otherwise, without prior permission of the publisher.

For Ian Patterson

Body & Soul

This is a tale of boilers and of souls, of devilment,
more impossible than implausible, a mannered stretch
of harking back. It hovers between two souls and four minds.
Let's slacken the line and reel in some grounding biograph.
André Revale and Terry Noblet were currants within
the cake mix of a nicely-bog-standard comprehensive.
In those days hard to tell apart, given that they were both
laughing terrains of pimples, sweating vats of virgin lust.
Their school blazers were currant surfaced. Duo-ed for German,
and History, leaning each-to-each, a pinnacled tent
of absolute idleness and Alfred E. Newman-style
nostalgie de la boue: they were in love with the lowest,
or wandering corridors crippled with corpsing laughter
at the sentence, "Nice though inn't she?" said through the nose Welshly.

James Russell

To chin-out-jut the lower teeth alternating with goof
of incisors was 'a yak-moose', while 'it's-a-fine-morning'
was to tuck the top lip like a bumper into the top
gum while staring into space, with a twinkle set in eye …
These were just two of their many faces. Not *The Prelude*
this, is it? No, not even a friendship. United by
what? The need to stave off adulthood? Let us draw a line
and say they were like disparate creatures tied by love of
foreign stamps or creepy crawlies. But why say 'disparate'?
André was smooth and Terry rough. André the fruit of loins
well laundered, an only child fretted over. Terry the
fifth of five housed in damp, squeezing blackheads to pass the time.
Reflect on André, the name, because one afternoon of
thought a dinner-lady and her tour-bus-driving hubby

chose that name for their up-coming son rather as a full-
back boots the ball right up the field expecting the team to
give chase. André was a lumbering prop-forward panting
after it. 'Terry' from the small kitty of Noblet names.
(One sister was a Terry too.) He used to be among
those who chanted to André: "Yrr name is fuckin' AnDREW."
Who pronounced 'threw' as 'threy' and 'glue' as 'glay' in front of him.
One day he decided he would live up to his banner
and did this all by himself, giving it the following form:
learning to like not the difficult, but the difficult
to like: Beckett's novels, the kind of free jazz where saxes
sound like boiling kettles, black instant coffee, *Disque Bleu,* crew
cuts, Dada poems, Disraeli's novels and his dress sense too.
It was a lot; it was his own; his jackdaw's nest or barn.

James Russell

There were still laughing days with Ter, but mostly he was shunned.
Evenings at home with John Coltrane and essays on Kafka
(Ed. Ronald Gray). Read hard, read and read and he got into …
a downward spiral? No, to Oxford University.
The sixth-form common room was tortured in his final months,
was on its knees, blood pouring from its mouth from the kicking
pride of André Revale. One lunchtime Terry and André
spent in a cider pub, where André talked of Kierkegaard
and they were thrown out for play fighting – serious play for Ter.
And later watching the cricket team one of them seemed to
flick a blade of grass in the other's face. A real fight now,
a gouging swift exchange in which, through swollen lips, the words
PEASANT and PONCE met in mid-air releasing something good
in their mist domain – an Indian summer, a friendship.

Body & Soul

Put a newly-hatched chick on a beach within reach of the
waves. Come on little one, you learn to fly right now. Whoosh, there
you go drowning again in your little commoner's gown
at dinner, tongue-tied, secretly failing to salivate.
When they could see that he was strong enough the wags of the
JCR called him Andrex, heralding a slide into
place, an almost smooth progression towards unconsciousness.
As students sloped about the sunny streets people were ill
in bed, too sick even for chocolates and chewing-hash.
It was the hot summer of those medium-strength emotions
he could have got at home until he met a perfect piece
of female life, perfect for him that is: tender and sweet,
wrapped up in a lecture on *Unto This Last.* She took, though,
the lead in all that counted, worked up a polish in him.

James Russell

Their married life seemed to begin the day after they met.
Try this: late 1950s-style songbirds in bromide-soaked
twin pullovers, with an "A" on one and a "P" (her name
was Pia) on the other; eyes shining to camera
or gaze-locked, each with a hand resting on a copy of
Woman's Realm or *The Radio Times*. **This** André would carry
Pia's books from school. Well, no … At a sign from her (grasping
his middle finger then a soft, slow pummel) they would nip
back home between lectures for a quick one at least once a
day. They could lean their sheets against a wall. People called them
'the long and the short straw.' But there was still the evident
'unconsciousness' of the preceding stanza: no more thought
of what he had than of gratitude in a shoaling fish
for its gills – which made its way into Pia's first novel.

Pia blackened pages with *Parson's Displeasure,* the first
of fifteen fictional works (title changed when she was sued
by Roald Dahl), while André smoked joints before their new TV.
Was this life's designated driver chained to a sipper
of cordial julep? No, wrong again. She fell pregnant
in her final year, her sure-thing First shipped to another
possible world. And André stopped swimming in smoky rings,
got a good degree and a job in publishing – thanks to
the contacts made by Pia's father in that actual world.
The past tense of 'thrive' jars to me (a crazy pull to 'throve').
Let's just say that thrive he did. Let's give this the shortest form.
Who wants to know about his management of the long lunch?
Who cares about her literary influences or lack of them?
A narrative thrust will push you into a muddy stream

of phrases like 'forty years on' and 'he did not repine'.
This is why people like philosophy, the skeleton.
Their skeletons changed not (need I say) through the forty years
and neither did their minds. He had the mental analogue
of arthritic knees, and her thoughts grew stiff above the keys.
But there was a resting line, a pure tone amongst the white
noise of their London life; and that is how we find them now.
A life softly punctate with Greens – Turnham, Richmond and Kew –
white tea in the sun, André's spare meticulous cuisine.
Indeed, he was a spare, meticulous man, measured, correct,
with a cool precision that his school mates once would have dubbed
android. But not (my motif!) so. *Nostalgie de la boue*
intact. Even Pia was ignorant. André himself
only slightly knew; but he knew his own activity…

Body & Soul

On Facebook, while Pia was fast asleep or typing hard
(have no fear, nothing cheesy here), he and his high-toned 'friends'
mostly shared posts from the in-theory Left, expressed intent
to go to poetry readings or wine-fuelled writer fests.
In fact he thought all modern poets were sad offsprings of
Yoko and Casaubon. He never went, not even when
one of his clients was reading poems (he thought he'd learned to write)
about his ex-wife and his latest flame. He liked the frank
or frankly drunk battings of views. But more he liked it when
someone posted photos of Russian dating sites, lets say:
posing with a Kalashnikov in one hand, a hoover
in the other, mini-skirted on a hearthrug side-by-
side with an enormous cod. That hit the spot for André.
One day after a bit of thought he tapped 'Yes' to a friend

James Russell

request from one 'Terrence Noblet, self employed'. He had seen
Ter once in the meantime – his first and last school reunion:
Terry in drunken anguish over his second or fourth divorce
only coming to himself by whipping up a chorus
of the school song in 4-4 time to drown out a disco
anthem. Retired early from school-teaching to eat and drink
full-time. Would Terry's posts be like the diary he kept
in the fifth form? Fantasies of Miss Smart agreeing, in
phonetically-spelt Yorkshire, to his utilising
her breasts in interesting ways. But self-abuse records
in the main. They had been reading one entry in Physics
('City lost 3-1, 2 wanks am; 2 after tea-time').
"Read it out Noblet!" the teacher had said. "Caught bus to school.
had fun at break. Went home on time watched *Crackerjack,* had tea."

A child of two could tell you this is the wrong kind of mud
to be nostalgic for. How could the 'Spirit of The Wank
Diary' translate into social media *jouissance* from a
man in his late 60s who was a belly plus some limb
and cranial adjuncts? But his 'Yes' had given to André a
stone that cried out to be turned over. Turned over every
day at least nine times. He opted not to see Ter's updates
on his own page, but dipped into his old compadre's posts
in the style of my unoriginal stone-turning-over
figure. The first motif was 'Eva-please-come-back-you-are
my-true-true-love'. But the thick thread throughout this was stacked food:
stacked before Eva; stacked before Terry alone in his
kitchen; and the thread through this double cream and curry sauce.
Eva's hard and unforgiving eyes above jumbo cod,

thrice-fried chips, a lake of mushy peas, a Yorkshire pudding –
a space craft landing in the planet of grease. Maybe a
stein of *weissbier* too. Somewhere there is a website packed to
the gunnels with spurious quotations. 'That which does not
kill me makes me stronger' (Nietzsche – What!). Well, Terry dug his
spade right into this and dolled them out to his Facebook friends.
Here is the idea: 'always look on the bright side of life'
(Arthur Schopenhauer), 'breakfast like a king, lunch like a
prince, dine like a pauper' (Hannah Arendt), 'Kinder, Küche,
Kirche' (Simone de Beauvoir). Here are the fish, the barrel
too … It was standard stuff, but sometimes falling leaves were like
gunshots to André. Fascinated he was by all these 'friends'.
They were ex-pupils … sorry, cringed André, *students*. Children
in fact. They lapped it up, and lapped up too Ter's cries for help.

Terry's GP advised a colonscopy after
a routine test. 'Please send out all your love to me. This could
be the Big C'. It was not. 'Could not have gotten [huh?] through
this without your support' … 'Yor a fiter Terry mate' (Faz).
'The Big C had a worthy opponent in you sir'! (Nodge).
Posing as a patient sage was also a stock in trade:
'Young friends! [a standard start] don't waste your lives, you must rage rage
against the dying of the light' … 'Yo cant say farer than
that Mister Noblet mate!' (Sharyn). And to think that this was
the Terry who in 1964 decided that
the clefts behind the knee afforded by a bandage on
said knee were ideal for holding a pen, chips, or forged card
for a dental appointment (all this André might have said
in his language of thought). He went to bed in gratitude.

A new partner for Terry. If André stood to their right
it would show "100." Round was young Kirsty Bailey, thumbs
flung up behind her latest plateful. Love was in the air.
Ter's seeming toothless grin (gnashers worn away by eating?)
adorned his posts. Of course, he taught her not so long ago.
Now they cohabited in oceans of *Blossom Toes* white
wine, and islands of his signature dish (chorizo, cheese,
kidney and Marmite pie). A simple photograph: table
back-grounded by his municipal-style garden, a box
of *Blossom Toes*, nibbles, and the words 'Ready for Kirsty
Bailey getting back from *Kwik Fit*'. No more gurning at the
camera in pubs: now beauty spots occluded by bellies –
theirs. The volume was turned up on all his gaudy updates.
Music posts plotted pre- and post- 'Kirsty Bailey' (Facebook

tends to force full names). Pre- 'Slittin' Wrists' by some no-hoper
punks; post – milky balm of lovey-happy… Of course, of course
I know, yes. Getting snagged on the barbed wire of Amisian
'de haut en bas' tacky larfs. Bogged in marshmallow rock drill.
But so in fact was André and for reasons good enough.
Happiness is good. But what do you do about a man
who shows it and tells it, photographs it all of the time.
And the surround … The blurred dog in the Bacon painting could
be chasing its tail for joy in sight of that dull and scratched
excruciating freeway squared by ruled vermillion.
Not in that surround no. Likewise, happiness could not live
(André's creed) in Terry's 'there'. It was greed by the wrong name.
Like some one else, André wished to 'be at least as alive
as the vulgar'. Terry and he were once vulgar in the

right way (bored with this yet?). When Tsai Chin's 'Good Morning Tokyo'
was a hit André and he strode down corridors singing
'I've got a boner' to that tune; and now here he was with
his working mouth and his 'young friends'. One night André had a
dream. Listening in a stone building with vaulted ceilings – forced
to listen – to harsh inhuman music played by seated
figures, seated before a vanishing pavilion
glowing with tapestries and towering candles always
flickering out of sight as the music made a fine grey
mesh like a place-mat in a chic restaurant. "Well that was
a rough night for you darling. Here. Kiss," said Pia to him.
"How do you know?" (accepting the kiss). "What you were saying."
"Which was?" (with intonation of a border guard's 'Ja und!!').
"Oh so literary," of course – "The Horror! The Horror!"

Body & Soul

André? I bet good money you are not warming to him.
Who would? Cold of blood, a long streak of water as running
fount of contemptuous, joyless, flim-flam? But you would like him
if you met. Devoid of people-fear he was, endlessly
interested in people's words, amused. Because there was
no fear there was no need to dominate. Got the idea?
It was a lovely-rare islet trait (tempting but silly
to make a parallel with Hitler's 'large, beautiful' eyes).
But there was fear, strong fear, elsewhere: when he would find himself
within the ambit of the engineered world. Of course, we're
within that ambit all the time. And so the deadly spores
of fear were in the very air breathed. For him the smooth of
civilized comfort had the smoothness of thin ice. Beneath,
behind were wires and valves and cogs, sprockets, pipes, taps, switches –

of which he knew nothing, of which he did not dare to know.
One mechano-spasm, one butterfly wing flap, and he
would be alone in a desert without water, broadband,
a nice cold Chablis, and warm toes. Plumbers, electricians
were for André priests of a mystical order. They knew
things, could do things, beyond the blue horizon of the world
between two covers. These two covers seemed to him a bed
for his valetudinarian self. One blown fuse or
spreading stain and the covers would be whipped off to reveal
the shivering weevil therein. Every household implement
was insured at least twice, but André could not steel himself
to raise the phone to his lips when something stuttered or blew.
That was for Pia. He took himself to cricket (summer)
or galleries (otherwise), then returned to clear water.

One morning – you would be right to think that this is where the
sort-of story sort-of starts, the dream kicks in, and the real
twaddle unravels – with Pia on a retreat, André
about to shave, the hot water left-lock poured stubbornly
cold. Explosive action, his Overground missed, he turned on
all taps persuading himself at each he had misperceived.
No. Hard fact. Crude fact. As his full-bloodied brain ticked over
the fact. Under D in Pia's file, *Dinky Peace of Mind*.
He struggled to sieve the fear from his voice, but his accent
returned (after all those years of 'I am not frightened to
jump that high'). An engineer would phone within 12 hours.
It happened in less than one; and André was comforted.
The 'Dinky engineer's' voice sounded almost middle class,
business-like, deferential, warm: "Bye then Mr Revale."

James Russell

Later … some comfort too in how he looked. "Like an FE
College Principal Lecturer" thought André. Tousled grey
hair, goatee, pressed fleece, pressed jeans (M&S?), but with the mere
homeopathic dose of 'What-am-doing-here-cum
How-am-going-to-handle-this'? Panic or distraction
in the eyes? André had no leisure to care, just wanting
it to end soonest. "Your pressure gage is on zero sir.
Should be inhabiting the zone [a hopeful-sly glance here]
Between 1 and 2." … "So what do we do then?" … "Well first sir
I figure out how to re-pressurise." … "You mean you don't
know already?" … "A rich variety sir, rich." He was
like a bear presented with a picnic hamper of faux
eatables, made in fact of wood. From the next room André
heard strange-limp archaic swearings: "Be reverent!" … "Crikey

Moses!" Or childish forms: "Oh bum!" Then, "Yep! Found it at last!"
He was called in to see the needle right at the top of
the desired "zone" – frighteningly near the red "zone" to the right.
"But what if it moves into the red?" ... "Reduce spending sir ..."
"Follow me sir." They went to the back of the house at once.
(This really is not Geoffrey Hill is it? Shall I relate
the day of the week, the weather?) The Dinky engineer
stroked the end of an outlet, showing André water, "You
need a new valve sir." I really must spare you narratives
of the next hour or two. The cloud of jokey panic, his
insisting on the front door staying open so he could
keep an eye on his van, asked for cuppas, failed to unscrew
the boiler's door then said it could stay on, or invented
relevant lyrics to ancient pop to mark his progress:

James Russell

"I'm tightening you now," to the Freddie and the Dreamers' song,
"I'm telling you now." Finally he told André, "This is
what you need to keep the pressure right in the zone: 8 mill
open-spanner." Leaving he shouted over his shoulder
"8 mill open, don't forget sir." The moment of throwing
yourself into a freezing wave is followed by a real
and welcome almost-warmth. In this case, for André, only
the first and with continuous aspect – a lasting shock.
It seemed as if the needle was creeping up. He could not
be sure. His iPhone photo-file was packed with images
of the dial. On the train back from her retreat poor Pia
opened André emails expecting grandchild photographs.
Dials are what she saw, and the constant sad refrain: "Darling!
Is this one higher than the last? Surely this one is? Huh?"

Pia returned in the evening to André in bed with
a bottle of designer gin and a carton of pink
grapefruit juice. She was not at all surprised, and fetched a glass.
Neither surprised that André could not go three hours (at night)
and 30 minutes (day) without checking. And she was not
surprised when, one sunny day, the needle wavered to red.
'Fey' is a good word, often used to mean effete or camp,
but I am pretty sure it means the weird light-headedness
of those about to die in all their kitch-sweet poetics –
'look at those twinkly-winkly stars, soon I will be among
their number. Trish has got a baldy?' – But André's near-fey
manner, post the red-region, did surprise Pia. "And will
the water run incarnadine, my precious puss?" ... "Shut up!"
she said as he sprinted straight to the phone, asking Dinky

for anybody but The Principal Lecturer. "He told you what?" said an Indian gent from Southall. "And what were you supposed to do with an 8 mill spanner? Use it as a good-luck charm?" This man reduced the pressure and showed him how to make the display digital (a well-earned rest for the iPhone). But – good God – the pressure still crept up. The gent returned, not only fixed the fault with confidence and charm, but fitted two oojahs called filling-loop taps so André could top the pressure up if it got low. Did André then relax? Oh did he hell. The checking then became for low, not high. "Does Dinky offer counselling?" smiled Pia to him. "Maybe The Principal Lecturer turns up with his couch?" André's reply was strained-unfunny fey. But in the days to come the fey was stowed and André returned to André.

This exposition from the sky, of course of course. Is it
the concrete or the iron reinforcing rods skewered
through it all? Is it like waiting for the army? Well one
more heave (epistolary exposition is to come).
André did love to dip his pen in acid and he had
a gift for it. And so, he almost salivated when
an email from *Dinky Peace of Mind* requested feedback
on his 'experience'. A varnished encomium to
the Southall gent dispatched, he set to work on *Principal*.
He started with ice: dispassionate recitation of
the facts, almost regretful and somehow *sotto voce,*
but with a brewing force till: 'at that point scores of rusty
Allen keys clattered through a split in his carrier bag
onto the counter to be refreshed by the spilling of

his third mug of tea'. It was then, André said, that he reached 'the inescapable conclusion' that this person was 'intensely incompetent' and that he surely must be a 'stain on the Dinky reputation'. *(Froth on the Daydream du jour?).* He pressed Submit, leaving himself sticky with an alien film … oh this was not his way. Cleanse himself with the mud-pack of Terry's latest update? "Still uploading your spleen? … Oh who's the fatty?" Perky Pia had popped up. André explained the background, foreground, and the murky froth of all of it. They sat and shared the ride down through that which does not bear repeating, and strangely it was Kirsty who drew Pia's attention, fascination even. "She's a photograph, a hologram, an inflatable doll … well." Laughter smoked around it: she looked identical in each.

There had been smooth weeks. André sailed along with 1.2
on the digital gauge. But then: a clickering between
1.2 and 1.1; a theatre evening soured
by this. Eventually, the 1.0, seeming-solid,
ghosted a 0.9, which sure-as-shooting then became
the quicksand of 0.9. André told himself he would
wait for it to settle down upon a round 0.8
as the Southall gent had initially been happy with
a flickering of 0.9 to 0.8. But no.
One day reading the paper in bed he knew that he must,
just must, like an elephant with musth, charge down stairs right now
and do the job. One quarter turn clockwise to open up
the filling loop and then another clockwise turn to a
tap letting water … gurgling … off, anti-clockwise turn.

James Russell

He swaggered through the house. He was responsible – yes he
alone – for a resting 1.3, gliding up to 1
.5 or 6 when firing. 'Cool', as his kids would say.
It was a cool but comfortable Friday night in June
when full of modest power he poured himself – he roughly judged –
between 3 and 4 units of a good Albariño
into a glass the size of a small dog's head; settled back.
"Nice one, André." The voice, a young clean voice, came from that chair
in the far corner of the room. No lighting there; but he
could make out not so much a shape as a blue wavering
sheen below the white lamp of a humanish head. "Pia!"
he yelled. "No need Andrew. I've frozen time. We're out of time
in a kinda special way." There was a quick hand-wave and
the room was in full light. Strange, is it not, that even when

in the grip of abject terror cool judgemental thoughts slice
through. This did not work, thought André, in K. Amis' *Green
Man* and it's not working now. Second, the notion that here
was an estate agent's stunt. The man he could see was the
central tendency of the blunt young blades from Foxtons and
the rest who came to his door to tell him what properties
in his area were going for: the suit too tight, the hair
obsessively parted beside a motionless quiff, a
Windsor knot that would not fit in his wine glass, long, long shoes.
But this tight suit seemed made of mackerel skin. It did not catch
the light so much as generate a blue/magenta glow
from within. "Call me Jonny," he said. "Now please just relax."
André did not trust himself to speaking without squeaking
in a whisper. "I'm so glad, Andy, that all's well with the

James Russell

pressure, but, tell you the truth, I'm here re that kind of thing.
You wrote to Dinky on the 23rd and I am sad
to say that Joel – the first chap you saw – is one of ours."
"What's ours?" André had found his normal voice. "And what are you?"
"Yes, indeed, I am a kind of 'agent' – we read thoughts too
you see – an agent of the Devil. A junior toiler.
As junior as I look, only twenty thousand years old.
Joel is merely a signed-up supporter; but we don't
like it when supporters get, let's say, the ordure end of
the stick. Thanks to you Dinky gave him the sack and so now
he's on the dole. OK for you in your residence and
priggish blinking white wine sipping. Sorry! Centre, Jonny.
Calm. Yes. Andy, I'll come straight to the point. We have lost power
and can no longer take souls; but we can *swap* them buddy.

Make no mistake, my brindle chum. Sorry! Jonny, centre.
Breathe, breathe." As in his acid-dropping days André felt his
sole option was to go along with this, bracketing, as
some put it, the whole question of 'what's-real-and-what-is-not'.
A sixth form disputatiousness surfacing he then said:
"OK Jonny, two things: these supporters, how does it work;
and what can soul-swapping mean? Surely it can only mean
brain swappage?" … "First, very simple. From word of mouth, from the
dark web, never from indoctrination, people appear,
like Joel, who not only like to inflict pain, and cause,
well, a blinking mess, but see it as their duty so to
do. Look around you at the peopled world. Are these no more
than bunglers? There's a lot of it about, to coin a clause.
Second, here's a lesson on what's within. The self's no more

James Russell

than a carapace of neurogloop, of import equal
to having smelly feet or nicotined fingers. The soul's
not that. It's not a bunch or traits and memories. It has
no properties. Imagine someone says he has a soul
that's extravert, or conscientious, neurotic or 'cool':
you'd laugh, and I know you." André, forgetting where he was,
Put in, "How can something exist devoid of properties?"
"Look at the place over there where the peonies are vased.
Anything could be there, a place-holder quite literally;
but the place exists alright. Now for a rather subtle
point: as someone who excelled at *Piers Ploughman* and not at
conceptual graft, you'll need for me to go slowly. Sorry
Andy, just telling it like it is. Good and evil are
not properties as such: they are things of which a soul can

have more or less. Speaking personally for myself (as
Benny Hill used to say) I have loads of evil, almost
no good at all. It's great – exciting – by the way." … "You've failed
to draw a line. What you call soul is no more than – what should
one say – the true self." … "Andy, Andy, Andy…" As Jonny's
shrieking laughter threatened to crack glass his image became
unstable, flip-flopping between that of a shark and of
a little girl. "The true self. The troooo true self. Oh dear, oh
very dear. 'Perspectives on the true self' – module Psy10,
a lecture series by Professor Roger Todger as
Scheherazade Payne-Whitebait and her friends attend, take notes.
Such worble words, those creamy globs of hopeful pus, those tin
properties of the University of Dingley Dell.
Cants!!! So sorry And." Jonny stood or floated up. "Breathe, breathe

centre. Back to my own lecture. Good and evil are the only things that fill the Plato mould. For they live beyond the mind in an objective realm, as friendliness and funk do not. They are strong magnets too so they can draw iron-filing radiants that seem a self; but are not. Are *not*!"
Gaining confidence from perceived waffle André spoke:
"Well, if I'm right the swap won't work. There is the acid test."
For the first time Jonny's smile dropped. Worse than the shark, his face.
"I would not advise cockiness dear sir. I can make it very difficult for you – or easy. Just settle your prickly person. I am not a bad trip. I am the worse that can happen to you. Now, I expect you're wondering who (and don't mentally correct my grammar) I'm going to swap you with …" It had not occurred to André. Nothing occurred

at all to his shrinking mind. "Mister Terry Noblet is
The One. Your soul will sit inside this hard-to-envy man.
Hallelujah! And he will be the soul who sleeps beside
the admirable Pia. Now what has old Terry done
to frame this symmetry? You'll find out soon enough; though you
will have to, in your kind of words, bracket off the 'you' as
the subject of the verb to find out." An explosive, high
giggle at this point. "Lets just say that Kirsty's ex lines up
with our Joel … And now stand up!" He did, and as he did
Jonny passed before him with a kind of grace, wielding what could
have been an inhaler, but was not one. A puff from it
up André's nose and he became a happy flower in the
sun singing to himself, "How can you teeelll a Joey? J…
-O-E-Y, Joey?" (Sung by Teddy Boys in his home town).

James Russell

As the happy flower of André drooped and burbled Jonny
grabbed him by one ear and up they shot from Gunnersbury.
How to tell what it was like to be André at this point?
Let's say he was just presentations minus the 'I think'
that is supposed to go along with them. Looking down at
The M4 the words of Marlene Dietrich in Paris
present to him: rubies travel up the long boulevard
with diamonds moving down to me. In fact they soon veered North
to Gloucester, landing in the car park of a pub called the
Turtle's Head (not the Koran this is it? But never mind).
André saw smoker-drinkers watching as Jonny eared him
down the cellar steps, but the relevance of this to him
did not arise. More interesting was repetition
of the words, "hello, and welcome to fascinating facts."

Body & Soul

What smoker-drinkers saw – a dapper blade in a sharkskin
suit leading someone with a bad debt down for a duffing
up. It happened a lot at the Turtle. How could they know
this was a procedure of Satanic psychophysics?
I will explain: you will have heard of the machine at CERN –
The Large Hadron Collider – a circular tunnel in
which particles accelerated from opposite ends
smash into each other to release smaller particles.
In this case, though, we have a straight tunnel underground and
as long as Gloucestershire in which it's persons, not small bits,
that speed to meet one another. And the meeting is not
a smashing but like an exchange of batons, the batons
being selves and that which travels straight on being the souls.
It's done by spinning. André is set spinning in Gloucester.

James Russell

While a few miles north Terry's set spinning too. They spin
at unimaginable speeds, travel at speeds of the
same unimaginable kind. The instantiations
of selves snag, tug, *return* and by a process known only
to experts in Satanic psychophysics (but not to
me) they are exchanged: with soul-Terry travelling south within
the André self; as soul-André moves north within the self
of Terry. By 'self' is meant body-brain: so memories
and all the dispositions. Given this, what was returned
to Gunnersbury was what I shall call Faux-André (André
with Terry's soul) and what was dragged back down to Bridgewater
was Faux-Terry (the Terry self with André's soul). And now
a rest from exposition. There has been too much. Too much
too of hectoring. Time to think of Kirsty and Pia.

The alarm rings, Kirsty thinks of the desktop computer
in the *Kwik Fit* office waiting for her. Cider, *Blossom
Toes*, beer were a bad mix but she can tough it up to get
the tea for her and snoring Faux-Terry. Later Pia
does much the same for Faux-André. Their lives run on unchanged
but with what you could call 'leakage'. The two men un-altered
to *eyes* of all but those who loved them. Kirsty and Pia
felt draughts, cold ribbons wrapped around their partners' desires
and doings. André still read Pia his never-to-be-
published letters to the ***LRB*** and the ***TLS,***
neither over-egged, nor over-stated and never right.
Terry still made the breakfast scrambled eggs his way: double
cream galore, a side of Maple-syruped pancakes and hot
chocolate 'to wash it down' (his favourite phrase). It did not wash.

James Russell

How could it wash? Look at what's washing underneath. Pressure?
Too much or not enough? Both. The high pressure of desire
and strong belief; the low pressure of what I called a long
way back (stanza 15) 'surround'. All these men loved, hated
thought and could not bear to think was quite intact but it was
un-embedded, without the soul-*setting*. You could not say
they felt unhappy. Unhappiness would be a boon: t'would
be theirs and recognised as such. André would lunch with friends
in Soho. Terry would see mates in the pub. The shows would
go on (rather as I am going on). It's not as if
what I describe is quite unknown to those who've never done
the Gloucestershire transit – that's no evasive metaphor.
With this mere décor, phenomenology cuts no ice.
Let's just say that if Jonny and his colleague in Bridgewater

could somehow tap – and I suspect they can – these men's waking
states they would perform the Devil's own high five. These two
lived inside the lyric of Bobby Darin's 'Dream Lover',
felt the ache of the irretrievable ghost referent.
It would be like seeking the source of a high wind that shakes
a tree, spending all day asking the tree, looking into
the perfect and wrong face of the woman who's next to you
knowing the ghost referent can somehow make it better
or less bad, or more real, more human; different would do.
"It's about time we pulled our fingers out … started thinking
about this here wedding Ter." Kirsty has spoken. And pull
them out they do. Faux-André sees the Facebook post and sends
the formulaic chuckle that if they do not invite
Pia and him he'll puncture all Ter's *Blossom Toes* boxes.

James Russell

Apart from fighting, and rugby maybe, the two now-fauxs had never touched. But Faux-Terry hugged Faux-André in a maximalist greeting while Kirsty smotherd Pia, in the Travelodge bar. Each man saw at once that a light was flickering out in the other while knowing that they must surf along on the wave of themselves and keep things as light as possible. Faux-André did this by the recycling of impersonations. His Will Self: in ghoulishly slow posh cockney: "If we wish collectively to imbibe some intoxicating beverages then one of us must then perforce visit that absurd ha-ha of a bar." Talk was what Faux-Terry did, ceaselessly, of schooldays, of obscure beat combos, and of food. He never listened, his face cracked open in a fixed grin." All sat amazed at pulsing joy.

Yesterday, Pia and Faux-André had driven up to
Nether Stowey competitively quoting Coleridge
as they went. It had been nice. But this ... *"C'est trés genial!"*
burst from a hyper Pia. "Who you calling genital?"
laughed Terry as their eyes met across the first *Blossom Toes*
bottle. That the wine tasted of boiled condoms mattered not
to Faux-André. Something was clicking into place, he hoped.
But later up in their room it was brown-out time. Plans for
tomorrow drily agreed – the wedding itself two days
away – and then some fitful sleep. Tomorrow night they would
meet again with the addition of Faux-Terry's best man
Clint, whose real name was Cyril, who was a cowboy or sorts.
In 1981 he'd done a Greyhound trip from East
to West and back, and had returned to Bridgewater transformed.

James Russell

"They're very laid-back over there," was his catch phrase. There, that must be him said Faux-André, next day. The London pair were were early to *The Laughing Horse*. Think William Burroughs, but with a pimp moustache and add a bootlace tie, pony tail and much more of the yee-haw dressing-up box. His speech strangely unstable between Texas and Somerset. They sipped their drinks in near silence, Clint's eyes hardly saccading from them. With Kirsty and Faux-Terry there they reached a rolling boil. Pia hung on Faux-Terry's many words, Faux-André turned his charm up to 11.5 in speech directed to Kirsty (yes!). And as for Clint, he was something between a shepherd and his dog. Clint raised his hand within a lull. They thought he was about to make a toast. Not that at all. "We must repair to the snug." … " 'Repair to.' What the fuck's got

into you?" was the Kirsty take on that. But out they went
to the lonely room overlooking the car park. Now Clint
spoke without accent and without gender it seemed to them.
 "I look at human history and think of the stopped clock
that is right twice a day. Somehow you got it right almost
the first time." Clint is speaking. "Yes there is God, Devil too,
souls and the rest. The rest includes daemons, one each of which
these chaps have met. I meanwhile am an angel." Early on
that night Kirsty had moved onto vodka and, anyway,
she had her share of devilment. Then not believing what
she would say then said loud, "You're no angel. You're a tosser!"
The words were more than enough. Clint told them what had been done
by 'the other side'. Three of them were torn between "well this
explains ..." and "So, what happens now? ... So, what does happen now?"

"Nothing. Our side does not do Disney tricks. Accommodate is what you all must do." At this he wavered in his seat into the glowing image of a cabbage white and then was gone. The silence was not as deep as England, but it was deep enough to make Faux-Terry shy of breaking it. But break it he did, saying at last that they should split up by gender. Faux-André and he to the car park, 'the girls' should stay put. Picture the scene. It is nine, the setting sun is pinkening the light in the little room while through the window you can see the men at a rickety table, Faux-Terry swigging *Toes,* Faux-André tipping Prosecco into a half-pint glass. Then Kirsty speaks, "Well if you think that I'm gonna take on your Andrew you've got another …" Pia cut in, "The question simply is: who now goes home

Body & Soul

With fatty?" … "Andrew, he gives me the creeps: too thin, sissy,
all that literature quoting. As for my Terry I can
quote too Pee: 'Why don't we play cards for him she sneeringly
replied?' You know the rest." Pia was not playing at all.
"I love André body and soul, the former just because
it happened to be attached to the latter. The point I'll
make is just this: the Soul's The Man, who needs the pishy self!"
The door burst open and the men came in arms round shoulders
singing the school song. "Where's my little bird?" Terry sat down
and Pia came to sit upon his knee, his man-spread legs
just offering sufficient of a perch for her. Kirsty
looked towards Faux-André as if to say … 'well you know what'.
And so did he. He looks towards the ground in almost dark,
and in the calmest voice, the extreme of voices, said this:

James Russell

"Announced in slurred diction but it is a trumpet diction:
was ever grief like mine? The wrong trumpet, the proper time
the time of the slop of cat and dog. A disjunction of
earth and sky, of land and sea; and now the one that lies
within me, which is the grief of all. Credences within
a story that makes itself up as the physical plane
of foliage surrounding a non-existent rock which
contains the man within the man within the man within
the tale unreal. When the cock crows I shall be quite alone,
as the barely-existing characters move in kitchens
below. Suave corporate of the great indoors, a half bleached
Kandinksy will hang in my view, like a flag of freedom.
I'll think whose grief this is in vocal of a dying fall
then looking either side ask if it is a grief at all."